COOKING CLASS
GARNISHES
COOKBOOK

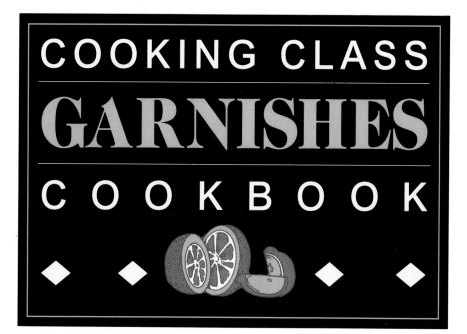

PUBLICATIONS INTERNATIONAL, LTD.

Pictured on the front cover (*clockwise from top left*): Chocolate Shapes (*page 62*), Strawberry Fan (*page 31*), Piped Cream Cheese (*page 91*), Caramel Roses (*page 78*), Butter Shapes (*page 86*), Scored Citrus Slices (*page 14*) and Sugared Fruit (*page 12*).

Pictured on the inside front cover (*clockwise from top left*): Lime Wedges (*page 23*), Bell Pepper Triangles (*page 42*), Chocolate Curls (*page 70*) and Tomato Rose (*page 46*).

Pictured on the back cover: Sifted Cocoa Design (*page 64*).

8 7 6 5 4 3 2 1

Manufactured in the U.S.A.

CONTENTS

Melon Balls with Leaves (*page 32*)

Chocolate-Dipped Fruits/Nuts (*page 80*)

Vegetable Ties (*page 44*)

CLASS NOTES

Making food look as good as it tastes is a goal of many cooks. Yet, many hesitate to add that special finishing touch that can make all the difference. If this sounds like you, this book is just what you've been looking for. Cooking Class Garnishes offers more than 50 creative garnish ideas sure to add that professional look to whatever you serve.

Page through this colorful selection of garnishes and discover just how simple it is to transform common ingredients, such as carrots, apples, gelatin and chocolate, into that extra-special accent. For example, colorful carrot flowers can add much-needed excitement to grilled meats. Or, delight your dinner guests with their own elegant apple swan. Need some help enticing little ones into eating their good-for-you salad? Gelatin cutouts are sure to guarantee a clean plate. And finally, nothing is more irresistible than a decadent cheesecake topped with an array of luscious chocolate curls.

The easy-to-follow step-by-step directions and how-to photographs included with each garnish make this publication as much fun to page through as it is easy to use. Whether a novice in the kitchen or an experienced cook, you'll surprise everyone—even yourself—with the professional results. To further assist you, our handy glossary lists many of the kitchen tools you'll need in order to re-create each of these eye-catching garnishes. And, to make your life even easier, we've included some time-saving tricks of the trade to further ensure foolproof results every time.

What's more, each fabulous garnish is rated as EASY, INTERMEDIATE or ADVANCED so you can gauge just how much practice or time it will take. Also included is a list of possible applications for the occasion at hand—whether it's the fanciest dinner, a children's birthday party or a casual outdoor barbecue.

If you enjoy cooking and presenting eye-catching dishes, then this publication is sure to provide you with hours of enjoyment. With a little practice, you'll soon be duplicating with ease those eye-catching garnishes seen in the finest restaurants and bakeries. So, grab your tools and get ready to garnish—there's no limit to your creativity.

SELECT THE RIGHT GARNISH
When choosing a garnish, pick one that enhances and complements the color and texture of the food. Use a bright garnish to perk up a light-colored food. Accent a soft-textured food with a crisp garnish.

Be sure to consider the size of the garnish as well. Team a large garnish with a tray or large platter of food. If the food contains a mixture of ingredients, keep the garnish simple.

Remember, garnishes should enhance, not overshadow or hide the food's beauty and flavor.

BEFORE YOU START
Look for fruits and vegetables that are evenly shaped, blemish-free and at the right stage of ripeness. In general, the firmer the fruit or vegetable, the easier it is to work with and the longer the finished garnish will stay fresh and attractive.

Be sure the knives you use are sharp. A sharp knife allows you to make precise cuts because it doesn't need to be pushed or forced. Sharpen your knives yourself with a sharpening steel or have a cutlery store sharpen them for you.

MAKE GARNISHES AHEAD
Whenever possible, make garnishes before you get involved in the final tasks of meal preparation. When you're giving a party, you won't have much time for creating garnishes at the last minute. (Be sure to store the finished garnish properly and add it to the food just before serving.)

•Most vegetable garnishes can be made ahead, then placed in airtight containers or wrapped in clear plastic wrap and refrigerated until the next day.

•To keep fruit garnishes fresh, wrap them in plastic wrap and store them in the refrigerator. When working with apples or other fruits that darken when cut, generously brush the cut surfaces of the fruit with lemon juice before wrapping and refrigerating.

•Place garnishes that need to dry or firm-up in a cool, dry place for several hours or overnight.

•For extra crispness, let chilled garnishes stay in the ice water an extra hour or two. Or, thoroughly drain the garnishes, then wrap in plastic wrap and refrigerate overnight.

TOOLS FOR GARNISHING

Just as you rely on the equipment in your kitchen to help you turn out a good meal, you'll also need a few tools to create spectacular garnishes. Here are some of the most common items:

Apple cutter/corer (2): This wheel-shaped gadget is great for cutting vegetables, such as carrots, as well as apples.

Broiler pan: For best results when broiling high-fat foods, such as bacon, make sure the pan you use has a rack with grooves or holes that allow the fat to drip down into a lower pan.

Brushes (11): Standard pastry brushes work for most garnishing, but for precise or delicate chores, a child's small paintbrush is best.

Butter curler, butter paddles and candy or butter molds (3): Each of these helps you shape butter. Use the curler to form delicate butter curls, the paddles for butter balls and the molds for special designs.

Citrus stripper (15): Use this tool to cut a thin strip of peel from citrus fruits or other fresh produce.

Cutting board: No matter what type of cutting board you have, be sure to keep it clean. Wash it with soap and water, then disinfect it with a mild solution of chlorine bleach and hot water after each use.

Decorating bag or parchment cone (7): Use these items for piping designs and other cake-decorating tasks.

Decorating tips (8): The tips you'll use most often are *writing tips, star tips, rose tips* and *leaf tips.* Start out by purchasing one of each type. Then add to your collection whenever you need an additional tip for a new garnish.

Deep-fat-frying thermometer: Be sure to use the type of thermometer that is designed to measure the high temperatures of cooking oil used in frying.

Doilies and stencils: These are used for transferring designs to tops of cakes, cheesecakes and other desserts.

Grapefruit knife (13): The jagged edges on this knife come in handy for many garnishing tasks.

Hand grater (4): A grater with at least one section for fine pieces and another section for larger shreds is the most practical.

Hors d'oeuvre cutters or small cookie cutters (12): These are sold in most cookware shops. Choose the shapes you think you'll use most often.

Knives (5): Sharp knives are a must. The knives you'll use most often are a *chef's knife* for cutting large items, such as watermelons; a *utility knife* for medium-sized foods, such as pineapples or cantaloupes; and a *paring knife* for all-purpose cutting.

Melon baller (14): This handy tool comes in a variety of sizes. The one that's the most versatile is the 1-inch-diameter size.

Resealable plastic food storage bag: For piping, select a bag with a self-closing seal that is typically used for freezing. The extra weight of this type of bag makes the task easier.

Scissors (9): A small pair is ideal for snipping small items, such as green onion tops. Kitchen scissors or poultry shears are better for large, tough jobs.

Skewers and toothpicks (6): For garnishing, keep a supply of wooden toothpicks as well as 6- and 10-inch wooden skewers on hand. Occasionally you may need a metal skewer. Choose one about 8 inches long.

Vegetable peeler (10): The swivel type works best—just make sure it's sharp.

Wire strainer or sieve (1): This bowl-shaped tool made from wire mesh is great for sifting or sprinkling powdered sugar or cocoa over foods as well as for draining foods.

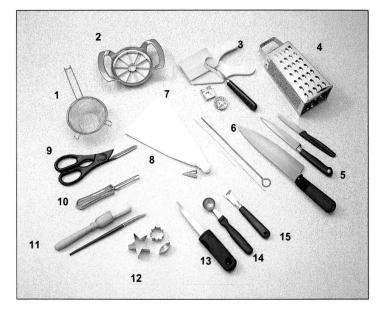

Fruit Garnishes

Sumptuous strawberries, zesty lemons and juicy melons are just a few of the fabulous fruits featured in this collection of eye-catching garnishes.

Apple Cups, 28
Apple Swans, 20
Cherry Flowers, 22
Citrus Cups, 28
Citrus Knots, 30
Citrus Loops, 15
Citrus Peel, Candied, 26
Citrus Slices, Scored, 14
Citrus Twists, 50
Fruit, Sugared, 12
Fruits, Chocolate-
     Dipped, 80
Lemon Butterflies, 18
Lemon Rosebuds,
     Candied, 10

Lemon Wedges, 23
Lime Butterflies, 18
Lime Wedges, 23
Melon Balls with
     Leaves, 32
Melon Fans, 24
Orange Roses, 46
Strawberry Fans, 31
Watermelon Basket, 16
Watermelon Bowl, 16

Clockwise from top left: Lemon Butterflies, Strawberry Fans, Melon Balls with Leaves, Cherry Flowers

Candied Lemon Rosebuds *(Intermediate)*

Serve individual slices of lemon meringue pie or chocolate cake topped with their own candied lemon rosebud.

For a special gift, trim a plate filled with lemon bars with several candied lemon rosebuds.

Crown a picture-perfect trifle with a cluster of candied lemon rosebuds.

Lemon
Sugar*
Water*
Tiny fresh mint leaves (optional)

EQUIPMENT:
Cutting board
Paring knife
Vegetable peeler
Wooden toothpicks
Small saucepan
Wooden spoon
Wire strainer or sieve
Medium bowl
Large slotted spoon
Shallow bowl (optional)
Teaspoon (optional)
Waxed paper

*You will need about 1½ cups *each* of sugar and water for each lemon.

1. Place lemon on its side on cutting board. Cut off ends with paring knife; discard ends. Starting at one end of lemon, peel lemon with vegetable peeler by cutting a continuous strip of peel in a spiral fashion around lemon, being sure to press firmly with vegetable peeler while peeling.

2. Place lemon peel on cutting board; cut into 4- to 5-inch lengths.

3. Scrape cut side of peel with paring knife to remove white membrane, being careful not to break strips.

4. Starting at one end of each strip, roll peel to form cone shape, tapering bottom as much as possible.

Step 1. Peeling lemon.

Step 3. Scraping off white membrane from peel.

Step 4. Rolling peel into cone shape.

5. Break wooden toothpick in half. Insert one toothpick half horizontally into base of lemon rosebud to secure. Repeat with remaining lengths of peel to make additional rosebuds.

6. Combine equal parts of sugar and water in small saucepan. Bring to a boil over medium heat, stirring constantly with wooden spoon. Reduce heat to low. Simmer 3 minutes.

7. Carefully add lemon rosebuds to sugar mixture.

8. Simmer 15 to 20 minutes or until peel is completely translucent.

9. Place wire strainer or sieve over bowl. Carefully remove lemon rosebuds from sugar mixture with slotted spoon; place in sieve to drain thoroughly.

10. If desired, add additional sugar to shallow bowl. Place rosebuds on top of sugar. Sprinkle a light, even coating of additional sugar over rosebuds with teaspoon.

11. Carefully remove wooden picks. Place lemon rosebuds on waxed paper. Let dry thoroughly. Arrange on desired food or plate. Trim with tiny fresh mint leaves, if desired.

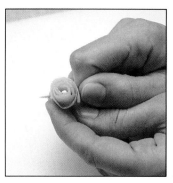

Step 5. Securing rosebud with toothpick.

Step 7. Adding rosebuds to sugar mixture.

Step 10. Sprinkling rosebuds with sugar.

Sugared Fruit/Flowers (Easy)

At holiday time, spruce up tortes, fruitcakes or steamed puddings with a cascade of sugared grapes or cranberries.

🐝

Trim a silver tray of elegant pastries with delicate sugared roses or geraniums.

🐝

Serve individual portions of baked custard, mousse or rice pudding with sugared violets.

🐝

For a cocktail party, arrange trays of sliced cheeses and smoked sausage. Trim the trays with an assortment of sugared fruits.

Grapes (in small clusters), cranberries, bing cherries and/or blueberries
Egg white
Sugar
Small nontoxic leaves (optional)

EQUIPMENT:
Paper towels
Small bowl
Fork
Small, clean paintbrush or pastry brush
Waxed paper
Teaspoon

1. **For sugared fruit,** wash fruit. Gently blot dry with paper towels or let air-dry on paper towels.

2. Beat egg white in small bowl with fork until foamy.

3. Brush egg white onto each piece of fruit with paintbrush or pastry brush, coating all sides of fruit thinly and evenly.

4. Place fruit on waxed paper that has been covered with sugar. Sprinkle a light even coating of sugar over fruit with teaspoon.

5. If any areas are not coated, repeat layers of egg white and sugar.

6. Let sugared fruit stand at room temperature until coating is dry. Trim with nontoxic leaves, if desired.

Step 2. Beating egg white.

Step 3. Brushing fruit with egg white.

Step 4. Sprinkling fruit with sugar.

7. **For sugared flowers,** substitute fresh small edible flowers such as geraniums, roses, nasturtiums, violets and marigolds for fruit and superfine sugar for granulated sugar.

8. Wash flowers. Gently blot dry with paper towels or let air-dry on paper towels. Beat egg white in small bowl with fork until foamy.

9. Brush egg white onto each flower with paintbrush, coating both sides of petals thinly and evenly.

10. Place flower on large sheet of waxed paper that has been covered with sugar.

11. Spoon additional sugar into sieve. Sprinkle a light, even coating of sugar over each flower. If any areas are not coated, repeat layers of egg white and sugar.

12. Let sugared flowers stand at room temperature until coating is dry.

Step 9. Brushing flower with egg white.

Step 10. Placing flower on sugared surface.

Step 11. Sprinkling flower with sugar.

Scored Citrus Slices *(Easy)*

A couple of scored citrus slices along with a sprig of fresh parsley makes an eye-catching garnish for your favorite fish.

Trim a Waldorf salad or any other fruit salad by tucking a border of scored orange slices around the edge of the salad.

To make a bowl of citrus-based punch or sangria look party-special, float scored citrus slices top.

Drop half of a scored orange slice into a mug and fill it with hot spiced cider—wonderful on cold winter days!

Lemon, lime, orange or grapefruit

EQUIPMENT:
Citrus stripper or grapefruit spoon
Cutting board
Paring knife

1. Cut groove in peel of fruit with citrus stripper or tip of grapefruit spoon, cutting lengthwise from stem end to other end.

2. Continue to cut grooves about ¼ to ½ inch apart until completely around fruit.

3. Place fruit on cutting board; thinly slice crosswise with paring knife.

Step 1. Cutting first groove in peel.

Step 2. Cutting grooves all around fruit.

Step 3. Cutting fruit into slices.

Citrus Loops *(Easy)*

Fill individual prepared meringue shells with lemon pudding. Top with a dollop of whipped cream and a lemon loop.

At your next dinner party, garnish the edge of each water glass with a citrus loop.

For an elegant luncheon entrée, serve crab Louis on lettuce-lined salad plates trimmed with a trio of citrus loops.

Lemon, lime or orange

EQUIPMENT:
Cutting board
Utility knife
Paring knife

1. Place fruit on cutting board; cut crosswise into thin slices with utility knife.

2. Cut each slice in half crosswise.

3. Carefully cut each half slice between peel and fruit with paring knife to loosen peel from fruit, cutting about *three-fourths* around the inside of the peel. (Fruit should remain attached to about one-fourth of the length of the peel.)

4. Holding free end of peel, carefully curl it under, tucking it up against attached part of peel.

Step 1. Cutting fruit into slices.

Step 3. Partially removing peel from fruit.

Step 4. Curling peel.

Watermelon Bowl / Basket *(Intermediate)*

A watermelon bowl filled with chicken salad makes an eye-catching centerpiece for an elegant backyard buffet.

Line a watermelon basket with plastic wrap; use to hold muffins or rolls.

Fill a watermelon bowl with cut-up fresh summer fruits for a quick dessert.

Well-rounded watermelon

EQUIPMENT:
Cutting board
Chef's knife
Long-handled spoon
Small drinking glass
Pencil
Utility knife

1. **For watermelon bowl,** place watermelon on its side on cutting board. Cut a thin piece from bottom of melon with chef's knife to create flat surface.

2. Cut off top one-third of watermelon; reserve fruit for snacking.

3. Set watermelon on the flat surface. Remove pulp from watermelon using long-handled spoon, leaving shell intact.

4. To scallop edge of watermelon bowl, place open end of drinking glass against melon so top edge of glass is aligned with top edge of bowl. Draw pencil line around glass edge to form scallop. Continue drawing scallops in this manner around melon.

5. Carefully cut along pencil lines with utility knife to form scalloped edge; fill bowl as desired.

Step 1. Cutting slice from bottom of melon.

Step 4. Drawing scalloped edge.

Step 5. Cutting scalloped edge.

6. **For watermelon basket,** place watermelon on its side on cutting board. Cut a thin piece off one side of melon with chef's knife to create flat surface. Set watermelon on the flat surface.

7. To make basket handle, start slightly off center of middle of melon and draw pencil line crosswise about one-half of the way down side of watermelon. Draw another line parallel to first to form strip about 2 inches wide.

8. Turn watermelon around; repeat pencil lines for other half for handle. Draw pencil line horizontally around melon to make guideline for top of basket. Cut along pencil lines for handle, being careful to cut only to horizontal pencil line indicating top of basket.

9. On one side of handle, cut along pencil line for top of basket, being sure to insert knife into watermelon pulp as far as possible. Carefully remove watermelon as piece is loosened.

10. Set removed fruit aside for snacking or another use. Repeat cutting on other side. Trim away pulp from under handle with utility knife.

11. Remove pulp from inside of watermelon with long-handled spoon, leaving shell intact.

12. Scallop top edge of basket, if desired (see steps 4 and 5). Fill as desired.

Step 8. Cutting along pencil lines for handle.

Step 9. Removing cut piece from melon.

Step 10. Trimming pulp from under handle.

Lemon/Lime Butterflies (Easy)

Having a Mexican fiesta? Garnish each dinner plate with a lemon or lime butterfly and your guests will say "olé!"

Add a flourish to baked cod or halibut by serving each portion with a delicate lemon butterfly.

Get the kids to eat their vegetables by topping each serving with a lemon or lime butterfly.

Lemon

EQUIPMENT:
Vegetable peeler or citrus stripper
Cutting board
Paring knife

1. Starting at one end of lemon, cut a thin strip of peel around lemon with vegetable peeler or citrus stripper. Repeat, starting at other end.

2. Place both strips on cutting board. Using paring knife, cut peel into very thin strips, each about 1 inch long.

3. Place lemon on cutting board. Cut off ends at place where peel has been stripped; discard ends. Thinly slice remaining lemon crosswise.

Step 1. Cutting strip of peel.

Step 2. Cutting peel into thin strips.

Step 3. Slicing lemon.

4. Cut each slice into thirds.

5. To make each butterfly, arrange two lemon wedges on desired food or plate, with points of wedges touching at center.

6. To make antennae, carefully place two strips of peel where lemon wedges touch.

Lime Butterfly Variation: Substitute lime for lemon; continue as directed.

Step 4. Cutting slice into thirds.

Step 5. Forming wings of butterfly.

Step 6. Adding antennae.

Apple Swans *(Advanced)*

Make an apple swan the focal point of a tray of hors d'oeuvres or finger sandwiches.

Create an attractive centerpiece with a family of apple swans floating in a shallow glass bowl half-filled with ice water.

For a breathtaking dessert at a dinner party, carve an apple swan for each guest and serve on a "sea" of rich chocolate sauce or stirred custard.

Large, firm apple
Bowl of lemon juice

EQUIPMENT:
Cutting board
Utility knife
Wooden toothpick

1. Remove stem from apple. Place apple, stem end down, on cutting board. Cut a ½-inch-thick slice off one side of apple with utility knife.

2. For swan head, place slice, flat side down, on board. Cut a piece shaped like a question mark from slice; taper one end to resemble beak. Dip swan's head into lemon juice; set aside.

3. Place remaining cut apple, flat side down, on cutting board, with stem end toward you. Working in center of the top, cut out a thin, shallow wedge with utility knife. Lift out wedge. Dip wedge into lemon juice; set aside.

4. Using a gentle sawing motion, continue cutting progressively larger wedges (each ⅛ inch larger than the last) for a total of five wedges.

5. Remove each wedge as it is cut; dip into lemon juice. Consecutively line up wedges on board.

Step 2. Cutting swan's head.

Step 3. Removing first wedge.

Step 5. Lining up wedges for back.

6. To carve a wing, turn remaining cut apple so one long side faces you. Angling utility knife slightly toward narrow end of apple, cut out a similar series of four ⅛-inch-thick wedges from side of apple.

7. Dip completed wedges into lemon juice. Consecutively line up wedges on board. Turn apple around. Repeat on other side. (If desired, cut out an additional series of two or three tiny wedges below each set of larger wedges for a more delicate look.)

8. Dip carved apple into lemon juice. Reassemble each set of wedges; place in cavities in apple.

9. Using your fingers or point of utility knife, slide wedges apart slightly to give layered appearance.

10. Insert half a wooden toothpick in bottom of cut swan head. Press head into center cavity at narrow end of apple to secure.

Tip: Apple swans can be made several hours before serving. Wrap completed swans in plastic wrap and refrigerate until serving time.

Step 8. Reassembling apple.

Step 9. Separating wedges.

Cherry Flowers *(Easy)*

Dress up a molded cherry salad by spooning a small amount of vanilla yogurt over each serving and centering a maraschino cherry flower on top.

Add a hint of color to individual servings of rice pudding by trimming with a maraschino cherry flower and a small sprig of mint.

For Christmas gift-giving, drizzle your favorite homemade breads, coffeecakes or cookies with powdered-sugar icing. Decorate with red and green candied-cherry flowers.

Maraschino cherry or candied cherry
Tiny piece of candied fruit or peel (optional)

EQUIPMENT:
Cutting board
Paring knife

1. Place cherry on cutting board. Cut into six wedges with paring knife, being careful to leave bottom ⅓ of cherry uncut.

2. Use tip of knife to gently pull out cherry wedges to resemble flower petals.

3. If desired, place tiny piece of candied fruit or peel in center of flower.

Step 1. Partially cutting through cherry to make wedges.

Step 2. Separating wedges to resemble flower.

Lime/Lemon Wedges *(Intermediate)*

Float lime and/or lemon wedges in a bowl of citrus punch.

❦

For an easy yet elegant dessert, place scoops of lime sherbet in pretty glasses; trim each serving with a lime or lemon wedge and a sprig of mint.

❦

Arrange two or three lime or lemon wedges in the center of a key lime or other citrus-based cream pie.

❦

Perk up a bowl of buttered rice or rice pilaf with a lemon wedge garnish.

Lime

EQUIPMENT:
Cutting board
Paring knife

1. Place lime on cutting board; cut in half lengthwise with paring knife.

2. Place fruit half, cut side down, on cutting board. Working in center of the top of fruit, cut out a thin, shallow wedge from fruit, being careful not to cut all the way into fruit.

3. Remove wedge; set aside.

4. Using a gentle sawing motion, continue cutting progressively larger wedges (each $\frac{1}{8}$ inch larger than the last) for a total of four or five wedges. Remove each wedge as it is cut.

5. Repeat with remaining half of fruit.

Lemon Wedge Variation: Substitute lemon for lime; continue as directed.

Step 2. Cutting a thin, shallow wedge from fruit.

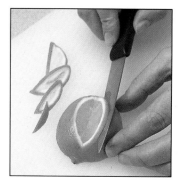

Step 4. Cutting progressively larger wedges.

Melon Fans *(Intermediate)*

Serve a scoop of chicken, tuna or shrimp salad on four or five melon fans arranged spoke-fashion on a salad plate.

Scoop assorted fruit-flavored ice creams or sherbets into a banana-split dish. Tuck melon fans next to scoops.

For a quick first course, place two or three thin slices of smoked turkey or salmon on a small plate. Garnish with a melon fan.

Cantaloupe or honeydew melon

EQUIPMENT:
Cutting board
Chef's knife
Paring knife
Teaspoon

1. Place melon on cutting board. Cut off ends with chef's knife; discard. Cut melon crosswise into 1-inch-thick slices.

2. Cut each melon slice into thirds with paring knife.

3. Remove seeds with spoon; discard seeds.

4. Remove peel from melon pieces with paring knife; discard peel.

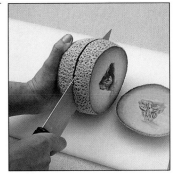

Step 1. Cutting melon into 1-inch-thick slices.

Step 2. Cutting slice into thirds.

Step 4. Removing peel.

5. For each fan, place one melon piece on cutting board with small curved edge facing you. About ½ inch from one end of melon piece, make a straight downward cut, being careful to cut only about two-thirds of way into melon piece.

6. Make additional straight cuts at 1-inch intervals until about ½ inch from other end of melon piece.

7. Position knife at first straight cut; make a slanting cut from there to bottom of second straight cut.

8. Remove small wedge resulting from this cut; set aside for snacking or another use. Repeat with remaining straight cuts.

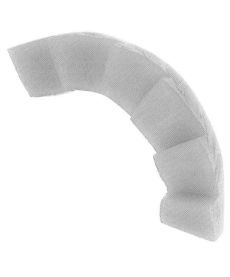

Step 6. Making cuts at 1-inch intervals.

Step 7. Making slanting cuts.

Step 8. Removing wedges.

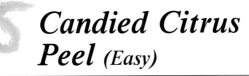

Candied Citrus Peel *(Easy)*

Tiny strips of candied citrus peel are the perfect topping for cups of Irish coffee, cappuccino or espresso.

When serving cake with a citrus filling, add some zing by trimming the top with strips of candied citrus peel.

Spoon apple or blueberry crisp into dessert dishes. Nestle a strip of candied citrus peel along the edge of each one.

1. Wash fruit; dry thoroughly with paper towels. Cut strips of peel from fruit with vegetable peeler.

2. Place strips on cutting board. If necessary, scrape cut side of peel with paring knife to remove white membrane.

3. Cut strips into very thin strips.

4. Combine equal amounts of sugar and water in small saucepan. Bring to a boil over medium heat, stirring constantly with wooden spoon. Boil 3 minutes.

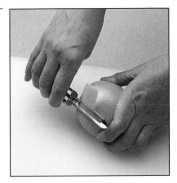

Step 1. Cutting strips of peel from fruit.

Step 2. Scraping off white membrane from peel.

Step 3. Cutting peel into thin strips.

Lime, lemon, orange or grapefruit
Sugar*
Water*

EQUIPMENT:
Paper towels
Vegetable peeler
Cutting board
Paring knife
Small saucepan
Wooden spoon
Wire strainer or sieve
Large bowl
Small resealable plastic food
 storage bag
Waxed paper

*You will need about 1½ cups *each* of sugar and water for each piece of whole fruit.

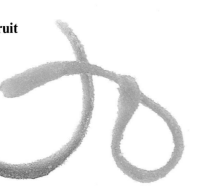

5. Carefully add strips of peel to boiling mixture.

6. Reduce heat to low. Simmer 10 to 12 minutes or until peel turns completely translucent.

7. Place wire strainer or sieve over bowl. Spoon strips of peel into strainer or sieve; drain thoroughly.

8. Add additional sugar to plastic bag. Add strips of peel; seal bag. Shake until evenly coated with sugar. Remove strips from bag; place on waxed paper to dry thoroughly.

Step 6. Simmering peel until translucent.

Step 7. Spooning strips of peel into strainer.

Step 8. Placing peel on waxed paper to dry.

Citrus/Apple
Cups *(Intermediate)*

When serving fish or seafood, present everyone with their own container of melted butter in a citrus cup.

For an inventive presentation, mound carrot-raisin salad into apple or orange cups; serve on a bed of lemon leaves or leaf lettuce.

As a first course for breakfast or brunch, serve a fresh fruit medley in grapefruit cups.

When the breakfast menu features a basket of bagels, serve whipped cream cheese in an apple cup right alongside.

Lemon, lime, orange or grapefruit (for citrus cup)
Orange or lemon juice (for apple cup)

EQUIPMENT:
Pencil
Teaspoon or melon baller
Paring knife
Grapefruit knife
Pastry brush (for apple cup)

1. **For citrus cup,** draw pencil line horizontally around center of fruit.

2. To use spoon or melon baller as pattern for scallops, place flat side of spoon against fruit so tip of spoon or top half of melon ball circle is above pencil line. Draw pencil line around spoon tip or top half of circle.

3. Continue drawing scallops around fruit in this manner.

4. Use paring knife to carefully cut around scallops, cutting to center of fruit with each cut. When all scallops are cut, carefully separate fruit to form two halves.

5. Cut around inside of fruit with grapefruit knife to loosen pulp. Carefully remove pulp, leaving shells intact; reserve pulp for snacking or other use. Fill cups as desired.

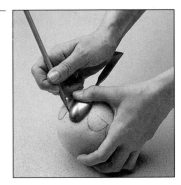

Step 3. Drawing scallop pattern around fruit.

Step 4. Cutting scalloped edge.

Step 5. Removing pulp from shell.

Step 7. Cutting thin slice from bottom of apple.

6. **For apple cup,** substitute apple for citrus fruit.

7. If necessary to get apple to stand level, place apple on its side on cutting board and cut a thin slice from bottom of apple with paring knife.

8. For sawtooth edge, hold knife at a 45° angle and pierce middle of apple with tip of knife; insert knife halfway into side of apple.

9. Form upside-down "V" by making a second cut, inserting knife halfway into apple to end of first cut. Repeat cutting "V"s until completely around apple. Carefully separate apple halves.

10. Using grapefruit spoon or teaspoon, remove pulp from centers of apple halves, leaving ½-inch-thick shells; reserve pulp for snacking or another use.

11. Using pastry brush, brush insides of both apple cups generously with orange or lemon juice to prevent browning. Fill as desired.

Step 9. Making sawtooth cut around apple.

Step 10. Hollowing out center of apple.

Citrus Knots *(Easy)*

Step 1. Removing strips of peel.

Place a citrus knot on top of a lemon meringue, orange cream or key lime pie to give a hint of what's inside.

❧

Spoon orange or lemon sauce over individual servings of gingerbread and top with a citrus knot.

❧

Orange and chocolate are flavors that just naturally seem to go together. For an easy dessert, drizzle some chocolate sauce over peeled orange sections and garnish with an orange knot.

Lemon, lime or orange

EQUIPMENT:
Vegetable peeler
Cutting board
Paring knife

1. Wash fruit; dry thoroughly. Remove strips of peel from fruit with vegetable peeler.

2. Place strips on cutting board. If necessary, scrape cut side of peel with paring knife to remove white membrane.

3. Cut strips into $3\frac{1}{2} \times \frac{1}{8}$-inch pieces.

4. Tie each piece into a knot.

Step 2. Scraping off white membrane from peel.

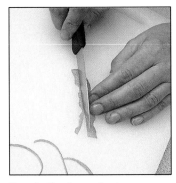

Step 3. Cutting strips into $3\frac{1}{2} \times \frac{1}{8}$-inch pieces.

Strawberry Fans (Easy)

Strawberry shortcake, one of America's all-time favorite desserts, is made extra-special when it's sporting a dollop of whipped cream and a strawberry fan.

Make cream puffs, eclairs or neapolitans all the more irresistible by tucking a strawberry fan or two at the base of each pastry before you serve it.

Nothing beats the summer doldrums like a strawberry shake made with fresh strawberries and topped with a strawberry fan.

1. Place strawberry on cutting board with pointed end facing you.

2. Make four or five lengthwise cuts from just below stem end of strawberry to pointed end, using paring knife.

3. Fan slices apart slightly, being careful to keep all slices attached to cap. Place on plate or food to secure in position.

Step 2. Partially cutting through strawberry.

Step 3. Fanning strawberry.

Strawberries with tops attached

EQUIPMENT:
Cutting board
Paring knife

Melon Balls with Leaves *(Intermediate)*

Create a decorative border of melon balls and leaves around the base of a cheese ball or molded fruit salad.

For a light dessert, arrange melon balls and leaves on individual dessert plates. Drizzle with strawberry or raspberry purée. Serve with macaroons or butter cookies.

For a summertime buffet, dress up platters of cold sliced ham and turkey with clusters of melon balls and leaves.

Top an ice cream pie or frozen mousse dessert with a grouping of melon balls and leaves.

Honeydew melon and/or cantaloupe

EQUIPMENT:
Cutting board
Chef's knife
Large spoon
Paring knife
Toothpick
Melon baller
Waxed paper

1. Place melon on cutting board; cut in half lengthwise with chef's knife. Scoop out seeds with spoon; discard seeds.

2. To make leaves, cut several thin slices from one melon half.

3. Remove peel from slices with paring knife; discard peel.

4. Cut leaf shapes out of slices with paring knife. (Small leaves should be about $5/8$ inch long and $3/4$ inch wide. Large leaves should be about $1\frac{1}{2}$ inches long and $5/8$ inch wide.)

Step 2. Cutting thin slices from melon.

Step 3. Removing peel from melon slices.

Step 4. Cutting out leaf shapes.

5. Score vein pattern in leaves, using tip of toothpick.

6. To make melon balls, place cup of melon baller against flesh of another melon half. Press firmly on melon baller to cut into flesh. Rotate melon baller until cup faces up.

7. Remove melon baller; invert onto waxed paper to remove melon ball. Repeat to make additional melon balls.

8. Place leaf on desired food or plate. Nestle melon balls against ends of leaves.

Step 5. Scoring pattern in leaves.

Step 6. Making melon balls.

Step 7. Removing balls from melon baller.

Vegetable Garnishes

Nothing beats a colorful array of fresh garden vegetables. Discover fun, creative ways to add flair to everyday fare with delicate zucchini butterflies, vibrant chili flowers, versatile bell pepper baskets and more.

Clockwise from top left:
Summer Squash Flowers,
Zucchini Flowers, Tomato
Rose, Bell Pepper Cup, Bell
Pepper Triangles

Carrot Flowers/ Stars (Easy)

Coax the children into eating their carrots by cutting the carrots into stars rather than simple sticks or rounds.

Accent a tray of finger foods by creating a "bouquet" of carrot flowers right on the tray.

Create colorful canapés by spreading crackers or party rye bread slices with your favorite cheese spread. Top with carrot flowers or stars.

Frost the top of a molded vegetable salad with a thin layer of whipped cream cheese. Then add a spray of carrot flowers.

Large carrots
Chopped capers or caviar
  (optional)
Chives or thin strips of green onion
  tops
Fresh cilantro or parsley sprigs
Halved pitted ripe olives

EQUIPMENT:
Vegetable peeler
Cutting board
Paring knife
Apple cutter/corer (for daisies)
Citrus stripper (for stars, optional)

1. **For black-eyed Susans,** peel carrot with vegetable peeler. Place carrot on cutting board. Cut off ends with paring knife; discard ends. Cut carrot in half crosswise. Cut out a thin, shallow lengthwise wedge from rounded side of carrot. Lift out wedge with tip of knife; discard wedge.

2. Give carrot a quarter turn. Cut out another wedge, as directed in step 1. Repeat turning and cutting two more times.

3. Cut carrot halves crosswise into ¼-inch-thick slices.

4. If desired, sprinkle chopped capers or caviar onto center of each carrot flower. Use chives or thin strips of green onion tops for stem and cilantro or parsley sprigs for leaves.

5. **For daisies,** peel carrot with vegetable peeler. Place carrot on cutting board. Cut off ends with paring knife; discard ends. Cut carrot into 1½-inch-long pieces.

6. For each daisy, set one carrot piece upright on board. Place apple cutter/corer directly over center of carrot piece. Press down firmly and evenly, stopping about ½ inch from bottom.

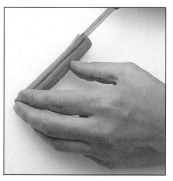

Step 1. Cutting shallow lengthwise wedge in carrot.

Step 3. Cutting carrot crosswise into slices.

Step 6. Partially cutting through carrot with apple cutter/corer.

7. Using your thumbs, push down on carrot piece as you remove apple cutter/corer.

8. Carefully cut out center core of carrot at the base with tip of paring knife. Fill center of each daisy with an olive half.

9. **For stars,** peel carrot with vegetable peeler. Place carrot on cutting board. Cut off carrot with paring knife where carrot begins to have a diameter of less than $1/2$ inch; discard thin end. Cut off stem end of carrot; discard. Standing carrot on wide flat end, cut a thin lengthwise slice from one side of carrot piece.

10. Repeat four more times, turning carrot slightly after each cut, to make a pentagon shape with five equal sides.

11. Cut a groove in center of each flat side using citrus stripper or tip of vegetable peeler. Cut carrot crosswise into thin slices with paring knife to form stars.

Step 8. Cutting out core of carrot.

Step 10. Cutting carrot into pentagon shape.

Step 11. Cutting groove in each flat side with citrus stripper.

Zucchini/Summer Squash Butterflies *(Intermediate)*

A dish of plain sliced tomatoes can be a thing of beauty when it's accented by a zucchini butterfly.

Layer zucchini butterflies with orange slices—a perfect complement to a platter of roast duck.

Gently slip zucchini butterflies on top of bowls of seafood bisque.

Small to medium zucchini
Bowl of ice water (optional)
Alfalfa sprouts or bean sprouts

EQUIPMENT:
Cutting board
Paring knife
Fork

1. Place zucchini on cutting board. Cut off both ends with paring knife; discard ends.

2. To score zucchini, draw tines of fork lengthwise down zucchini.

3. Repeat scoring all around zucchini.

4. About $\frac{1}{8}$ inch from one end of zucchini, make a crosswise cut about two-thirds of the way into zucchini.

5. About $\frac{1}{8}$ inch from this cut, make another crosswise cut all the way through zucchini.

Step 1. Cutting ends from zucchini.

Step 3. Scoring zucchini.

Step 5. Making second crosswise cut.

Step 6. Trimming slice to form base.

6. Place slice, cut side down, on cutting board. Trim uncut side of slice about $\frac{1}{8}$ inch in from edge to form a flat base.

7. To open wings, stand slice on flat base; gently spread rounded sides apart.

8. If desired, place slices in ice water to soften so wings can be spread further apart. Remove; drain well.

9. Repeat to make additional butterflies.

10. Position each butterfly on desired food or plate. To make antennae, tuck two sprouts into one end of each butterfly.

Summer Squash Variation: Substitute summer squash for zucchini; continue as directed.

Step 7. Spreading wings.

Step 10. Adding antennae.

Fluted Mushrooms
(Intermediate)

Combine one or two fluted mushrooms with a sprig of watercress to trim dinner plates when you serve London broil or other beef dishes.

Cap the ends of chicken kabobs with fluted mushrooms.

Garnish your favorite pâté with several fluted mushrooms.

Large fresh white mushroom cap
Lemon juice in a small bowl

EQUIPMENT:
Clean, damp cloth
Paper towel
Cutting board
Paring knife

1. Gently wipe mushroom clean with damp cloth or rinse lightly with water. Gently pat dry with paper towel. Place mushroom on cutting board. Remove or trim stem with paring knife; discard.

2. With paring knife held at a 45° angle, begin at top center of mushroom cap and cut a thin curved groove to edge of cap.

3. Turn mushroom. Continue cutting out curved grooves, making a total of six or seven evenly spaced thin grooves.

4. Once all cuts have been made, carefully remove each triangular-shaped piece with tip of knife; discard.

5. To help keep fluted mushroom from turning brown, dip into lemon juice.

Step 2. Cutting first groove in mushroom cap.

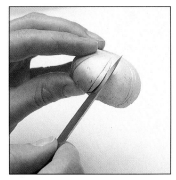

Step 3. Cutting additional grooves around mushroom.

Step 4. Removing wedges from grooves.

Cucumber Ribbons
(Easy)

Line the mold for a loaf-shaped pâté or cheese spread with several cucumber ribbons; fill mold with the meat or cheese mixture. When the appetizer is unmolded, the colorful strips will be on top.

Even ordinary meat loaf can be company fare if you dress it up by spiraling a few cucumber ribbons on the serving dish along each side of the loaf.

Baking a ham for a special meal? Slice the ham and place on a platter. Coil a cucumber ribbon here and there for a festive touch.

Medium cucumber
Bowl of ice water

EQUIPMENT:
Cutting board
Paring knife
Vegetable peeler

1. Place cucumber on cutting board. Cut off ends with paring knife; discard ends. Cut thin lengthwise strips from cucumber with vegetable peeler, making sure there is a line of green peel on both sides of each strip. Continue cutting strips until you reach seeds.

2. Turn cucumber, leaving about ½ inch of green peel before starting next strip. Repeat cutting of strips. Repeat turning and cutting once more.

3. If desired, trim edges of cucumber strips to straighten sides. Place strips in ice water to chill thoroughly. Remove from water; drain well.

4. Gently gather cucumber strips with fingers to form decorative ruffle. Place on desired food or plate to secure.

Step 1. Making cucumber strips.

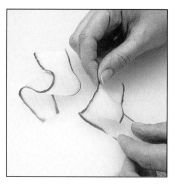
Step 4. Shaping cucumber ribbons.

Bell Pepper Triangles *(Easy)*

Float a bell pepper triangle or two on the top of your favorite creamy soup.

❧

Create an attractive accompaniment for steaks or chops by making bell pepper triangles using green, red and yellow peppers. Arrange a triangle of each color on each dinner plate along with the meat.

❧

Serve an appetizer dip with pepper triangles instead of chips.

❧

To dress up main-dish salads, arrange four or five pepper triangles on individual salad plates; top with a scoop of tuna or chicken salad.

Green, red and/or yellow bell pepper
Bowl of ice water (optional)

EQUIPMENT:
Cutting board
Paring knife

1. Stand bell pepper, stem side up, on cutting board.

2. Cut a slice, about ¼ inch thick, off each side of pepper with paring knife.

3. Remove membrane and seeds; discard.

4. Cut each pepper slice into a rectangle 1¼ inches long and ¾ inch wide.

Step 2. Cutting off sides of pepper.

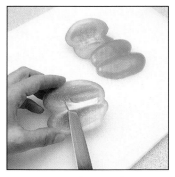
Step 3. Removing membrane and seeds.

Step 4. Cutting rectangles.

5. Starting one-third of the way from one long side of each rectangle, cut down remaining length of rectangle, ending ¼ inch from other end.

6. Turn rectangle around; repeat on other side.

7. To make each triangle, hold the two outer corners of a rectangle and bring both corners to center.

8. Overlap ends to secure. If desired, place triangles in ice water to crispen. Remove; drain well.

Step 6. Making cuts in rectangle.

Step 7. Twisting cut rectangle to shape into triangle.

Step 8. Overlapping ends to secure triangle.

Vegetable Ties *(Easy)*

Bundles of vegetables tied with onion or leek strips are ideal for buffet-serving. Guests can place the bundles on their plates quickly and easily.

❧

To dress up a dinner plate of turkey slices with gravy, use vegetable ties to secure individual servings of whole green beans.

❧

For a meal that is as pleasing to the eye as it is to the palate, team tied vegetable bundles with garlic-buttered shrimp.

Green onion tops
Large saucepan of boiling water
Bowl of ice water
Carrots

EQUIPMENT:
Cutting board
Paring knife
Vegetable peeler
Utility knife

1. Place green onion tops on cutting board. Cut tops lengthwise into ¼-inch-wide strips with paring knife.

2. Carefully add strips to boiling water in large saucepan.

3. Simmer 30 seconds; drain. Place strips in ice water to cool. Remove; drain well. Set aside.

4. Peel carrots with vegetable peeler. Place on cutting board. Cut off ends with utility knife; discard ends. Cut carrots crosswise into 4-inch pieces.

5. If desired, cut a thin lengthwise slice from carrot to prevent carrot from rolling as you make additional cuts; discard slice. Place carrot, cut side down, on cutting board. Cut each piece lengthwise into ¼-inch-thick slices.

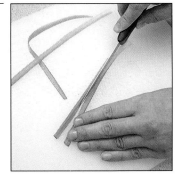

Step 1. Cutting green onion tops into strips.

Step 2. Adding strips to boiling water.

Step 4. Cutting carrot into 4-inch lengths.

6. Cut ¼-inch-thick slices lengthwise to make thin, julienne sticks.

7. Carefully add julienne sticks to boiling water in large saucepan. Simmer 1 minute; drain well. Place carrot sticks in ice water to cool thoroughly. Remove from water; drain well.

8. Cut green onion strips crosswise into 6-inch lengths.

9. For each bundle, place green onion strip on cutting board. Place 10 to 15 julienne carrot sticks crosswise on strip. Tie strip securely around sticks.

Green Bean Bundles Variation:
Substitute fresh whole green beans for julienne carrot sticks. Trim beans and prepare as directed in step 7 for carrots. Tie with green onion ties as directed.

Note: Substitute leek tops for green onion tops.

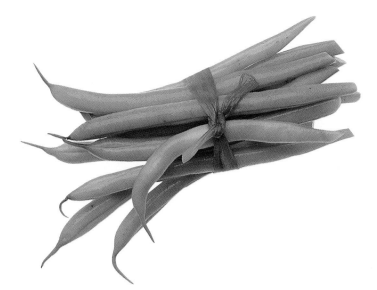

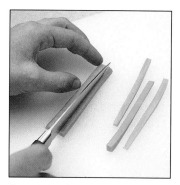

Step 6. Cutting carrots into julienne sticks.

Step 7. Adding carrot sticks to boiling water.

Step 9. Tying bundles.

Tomato/Orange Roses *(Intermediate)*

A delicate tomato rose is just the thing for adding some spark to a simple bowl of cottage cheese.

As a party centerpiece, create a nosegay of several orange roses. Arrange them in a pretty shallow bowl with orange or lemon leaves.

Is fettucine Alfredo your idea of culinary bliss? Make it a notch better by adding a tomato rose.

When serving a large whole fish, add a little color to the platter with orange roses.

Firm, ripe tomato
Tiny fresh mint leaves (optional)

EQUIPMENT:
Cutting board
Paring knife
Vegetable peeler (for orange rose)
Toothpicks (for orange rose)

1. **For tomato rose,** place tomato on cutting board. Cut a very thin slice from bottom of tomato with paring knife; discard slice.

2. Starting at top of tomato, peel tomato with knife by cutting a continuous narrow strip of peel in a spiral fashion horizontally around entire tomato, using a gentle sawing motion.

3. Place strip, either flesh or peel side up, on cutting board. Starting at end of strip where you started cutting, wrap strip around itself to form a coil.

4. Tuck end of strip underneath coil to secure. Tuck two or three mint leaves at base of rose, if desired.

Step 2. Peeling tomato.

Step 3. Wrapping peel into coil.

Step 4. Tucking end of strip under coil to secure.

6. **For orange rose,** substitute orange for tomato. Remove peel as directed, substituting vegetable peeler for paring knife, being sure to press firmly with peeler as you peel.

7. Starting at end of strip where you started cutting, wrap strip around itself to form a coil. Continue wrapping peel tightly around this coil, tapering bottom as much as possible.

8. Insert one or two toothpicks horizontally into base of orange rose to secure.

9. Place orange rose on desired food or plate. Trim with mint leaves, if desired.

Step 6. Peeling orange.

Step 7. Wrapping peel into coil.

Step 8. Securing base of rose with toothpick.

Carrot Knots
(Intermediate)

Crown the top of a nut-coated or parsley-coated cheese ball with a festive carrot knot.

❧

Add pizzazz to humdrum fish portions by brushing the cooked fish with butter or margarine and topping with a carrot knot.

❧

Stir-frying tonight? Sprinkle a carrot knot or two over each serving for a special touch.

Medium carrot
Small saucepan of boiling water
Bowl of ice water

EQUIPMENT:
Vegetable peeler
Cutting board
Chef's knife
Paring knife

1. Peel carrot with vegetable peeler. Place carrot on cutting board. Cut off ends with chef's knife; discard ends.

2. Cut carrot crosswise into 6-inch pieces.

3. If desired, cut a thin lengthwise slice from carrot to prevent carrot from rolling as you make additional cuts; discard slice. Place carrot, cut side down, on cutting board. Cut lengthwise into 1/8-inch-thick slices.

4. Cut each slice lengthwise to make thin, julienne sticks.

5. Carefully add julienne sticks to boiling water in small saucepan. Simmer 1 minute; drain well. Place carrot sticks in ice water to cool thoroughly. Remove sticks from water; drain well.

Step 3. Cutting thin lengthwise slice from carrot piece.

Step 4. Cutting carrots into julienne sticks.

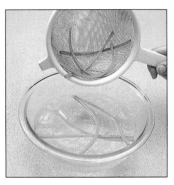
Step 5. Adding carrot sticks to boiling water.

6. To make each knot, use two cooked carrot strips. Shape each stick into a loop.

7. Insert top of first loop partway through second loop. Then insert ends of second loop around and through top part of first loop.

8. Carefully pull on both sets of ends to tie knot. If desired, trim ends at an angle with paring knife.

Step 6. Shaping 2 sticks into loops.

Step 7. Inserting ends into loops.

Step 8. Pulling ends to form knot.

Cucumber / Citrus Twists *(Easy)*

Brighten creamy chicken fricassee with a citrus twist.

Twist a slice of cucumber and slip it onto a platter of pan-fried pork chops.

Make a cucumber twist the center of an antipasto tray. Surround it with salami or ham slices, cheese cubes, hard-cooked egg wedges and olives or peppers.

Small cucumber

EQUIPMENT:
Cutting board
Utility knife

1. Place cucumber on cutting board. Cut off ends of cucumber with utility knife; discard ends. Diagonally cut cucumber into thin slices.

2. Cut slit through each slice just to center.

3. Holding each slice with both hands, twist ends in opposite directions. Place on plate or desired food to secure.

Citrus Twist Variation: Substitute lemon, lime or orange slices for diagonally cut cucumber slices; continue as directed.

Step 1. Cutting cucumber into thin diagonal slices.

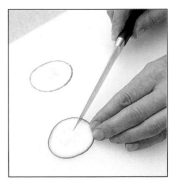

Step 2. Cutting slit in cucumber slice.

Step 3. Twisting cucumber slice.

Chili Flowers
(Intermediate)

Spruce up a plate of nachos or a layered Mexican dip with a couple of chili flowers.

Ladle up heaping bowls of gumbo or your favorite main-dish soup or stew and tuck a chili flower in at the side.

A chili flower is the perfect garnish for just about anything Oriental. How about trying it with sweet-and-sour pork?

Small red, yellow or green chili pepper or jalapeño pepper
Bowl of ice water

EQUIPMENT:
Plastic or rubber gloves
Cutting board
Paring knife

1. Because oils from hot peppers can burn your skin, wear plastic or rubber gloves when working with peppers. Place pepper on cutting board. Cut off narrow tip with paring knife; discard tip.

2. For each flower, start at tip of one pepper and make thin, lengthwise cut toward stem, making sure not to cut all the way through stem end. Repeat making lengthwise cuts all around pepper.

3. Rinse pepper under cold running water to remove seeds.

4. Place pepper in ice water. Refrigerate several hours or until pepper opens. Remove from water; drain well.

Step 1. Cutting off tip of pepper.

Step 2. Making lengthwise cuts in pepper.

Step 3. Rinsing pepper to remove seeds.

Radish Fans *(Easy)*

Add radish fans to your next tossed green salad.

Team a radish fan with some fresh basil leaves; use to trim a dinner plate of chicken cacciatore.

For a party, dress up a plate of nachos with a radish fan along with a sprig of parsley.

Large radish
Bowl of ice water

EQUIPMENT:
Cutting board
Paring knife

1. Place radish on cutting board. Cut off top and bottom tip of radish with paring knife; discard.

2. Cut parallel ⅛-inch-thick crosswise slices about three-quarters of the way into radish, making sure not to cut all the way through radish.

3. Place radish in ice water. Place in refrigerator several hours or until radish fans out. Remove; drain well.

Step 1. Cutting off ends of radish.

Step 2. Partially cutting through radish to make thin slices.

Carrot Curls *(Easy)*

Perk up a bowl of rice pilaf by trimming it with several carrot curls.

Turn an ordinary club sandwich into a company combo by spearing it with a small wooden skewer laced with a carrot curl.

Add color to broth-based soups by floating a carrot curl in each serving.

Large carrot
Bowl of ice water

EQUIPMENT:
Vegetable peeler
Cutting board
Paring knife
Toothpicks or small skewers

1. Peel carrot with vegetable peeler. Place carrot on cutting board. Cut off ends with paring knife; discard ends.

2. Cut paper-thin lengthwise strips from carrot with vegetable peeler.

3. Roll up strips into curls; secure with toothpicks or small skewers. Place carrot curls in ice water to chill thoroughly. Remove from water; drain well.

4. Carefully remove toothpicks or skewers before using.

Step 1. Cutting off ends of carrot.

Step 2. Peeling thin strips from carrot.

Step 3. Securing curl with toothpick.

Zucchini/Summer Squash Flowers *(Easy)*

Bring a heaping platter of spaghetti and meatballs to the table complete with a zucchini flower or two.

🦐

Accent the center of a spinach or broccoli quiche with a zucchini or summer squash flower.

🦐

For an elegant Oriental appetizer, arrange one or two egg rolls on a dish with side-by-side pools of sweet-and-sour and mustard sauces. Round out the dish with a zucchini or summer squash flower.

Zucchini

EQUIPMENT:
Cutting board
Paring knife
Vegetable peeler
Wooden toothpicks

1. Place zucchini on its side on cutting board. Cut off both ends with paring knife; discard ends.

2. Cut thin lengthwise slices from zucchini with vegetable peeler, making sure there is green peel on both sides of each strip. Continue cutting slices until you reach seeds.

3. Turn zucchini, leaving about ½ inch of green peel. Repeat cutting of slices. Repeat turning and cutting once more.

4. Cut ends off slices with paring knife to make even.

5. Make additional cuts about ¹⁄₁₆ inch apart along one long edge of each slice, cutting almost to opposite edge.

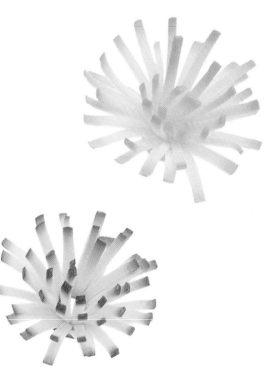

Step 2. Cutting thin slices with vegetable peeler.

Step 3. Cutting thin slices from third side of zucchini.

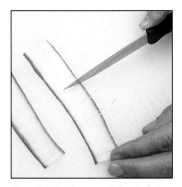

Step 5. Making partial cuts into long side of zucchini slice.

6. Roll up each slice from one short end.

7. Insert small piece of wooden toothpick through each base to secure rolls.

8. Set flowers upright; spread slightly to open.

Summer Squash Variation: Substitute summer squash for zucchini; continue as directed.

Step 6. Rolling up slice.

Step 7. Securing flower with toothpick.

Step 8. Spreading flower to open.

Green Onion/Celery Curls (Easy)

To make a chilled pasta main dish look elegant, serve it on your prettiest salad plates with a green onion or celery curl on the side.

Tuck a green onion curl into a bowl of barbecue sauce and let your guests use it to slather on additional sauce for their cooked ribs or barbecued beef sandwiches.

No Oriental meal is complete without a heaping bowl of rice. Dress up the bowl with a delicate celery or green onion curl.

Green onion or celery rib
Bowl of cold water (for green onion curl)
Bowl of ice water (for celery curl)

EQUIPMENT:
Cutting board
Paring knife

1. **For green onion curl,** place green onion on cutting board. Cut off roots with paring knife; discard roots. Cut onion crosswise into one 3-inch piece, leaving about 1½ inches of both the white onion and green top portions.

2. Make lengthwise cut from white end of onion almost to center of piece; repeat to slice end into thin slivers.

3. Place onion in cold water (*not ice water*). Let stand 30 seconds or until ends curl slightly. Remove from water; drain well.

4. **For celery curl,** trim ends from celery rib; cut into 3-inch pieces. Cut each piece lengthwise in half. Cut into slivers as directed in step 2 above. Place in ice water and refrigerate until ends curl.

Step 1. Cutting 3-inch piece from onion.

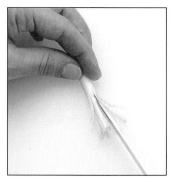

Step 2. Cutting end of onion into slivers.

Step 4. Cutting end of celery into slivers.

Radish Roses *(Easy)*

Team a radish rose with a sprig of parsley to add color to a creamy pasta salad or potato salad.

Slip a radish rose or two around the edge of a stir-fried dish.

Accent a bowl of creamed peas, beans or asparagus with a radish rose.

Radish
Bowl of ice water
Celery leaves (optional)

EQUIPMENT:
Cutting board
Paring knife

1. Place radish on cutting board. Cut off top and bottom tip of radish with paring knife; discard.

2. Set radish upright on cutting board. Cut a thin vertical slice partially down one side of radish with knife, cutting about three-fourths of the way into radish.

3. Make three additional slices down sides of radish, spacing slices evenly around radish.

4. If desired, make a second series of cuts about ⅛ inch inside the first set.

5. Place radish in ice water until it opens slightly. Remove; drain well. Trim with celery leaves, if desired.

Step 2. Cutting thin vertical slice partially into one side of radish.

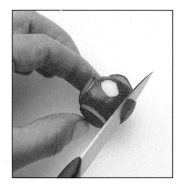
Step 3. Making additional slices around radish.

Bell Pepper Cup/Basket *(Easy)*

Use a pepper container in place of a bowl when serving creamy dips or guacamole. Or, use it to hold celery and carrot sticks as an edible centerpiece.

🍀

For an inventive presentation, fill pepper containers with single servings of tuna, egg or ham salad. Serve on a bed of red-tipped romaine.

🍀

Mold individual servings of tomato aspic in pepper containers. Serve them as a first course topped with mayonnaise or sour cream.

Large red, green or yellow bell pepper

EQUIPMENT:
Cutting board
Paring knife

1. **For bell pepper cup,** place bell pepper on cutting board. Cut about ½ inch around stem with paring knife; discard stem.

2. Remove and discard membrane and seeds.

3. Wash pepper under cold running water.

4. If necessary, cut a thin slice off bottom of pepper to create flat surface. Stand pepper up. Fill as desired.

Step 1. Removing stem end of pepper.

Step 2. Removing membrane and seeds.

Step 4. Cutting off bottom of pepper to make level.

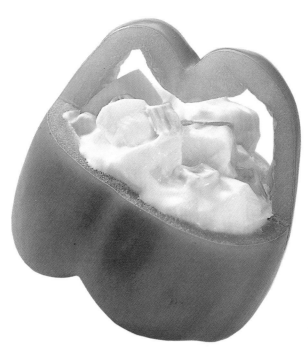

Step 7. Making 2 cuts in bottom of pepper to form "handle."

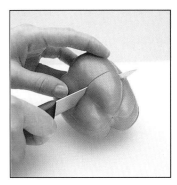

Step 8. Making horizontal cut to handle.

Step 10. Removing membrane and seeds.

5. **For bell pepper basket,** place pepper, stem end down, on cutting board. (Break off stem if necessary to get pepper to sit upright.)

6. Starting slightly off center, make a vertical cut from bottom of pepper just down to middle of pepper with paring knife.

7. Make a second parallel cut ½ inch from first cut, creating the basket "handle."

8. Make a horizontal cut from side of pepper to first vertical cut in pepper.

9. Remove piece of pepper. Turn pepper around; repeat on other side.

10. Carefully remove membrane and seeds from pepper with paring knife; discard. Wash pepper basket under cold running water. Fill as desired.

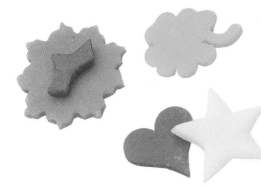

Sweet Garnishes

Add drama to everyday desserts with any one of these unbeatable garnishes. From intricate chocolate leaves gracing a caramel rose to whimsical gelatin cutouts atop cupcakes, you're sure to impress even yourself with each delightful masterpiece.

Clockwise from top left:
Gelatin Cutouts, Chocolate Cutouts, Feathered Icing, Gumdrop Bow, Caramel Roses with Chocolate Leaves

Chocolate Drizzles/ Shapes (Easy)

To dress up individual servings of pudding or cake, top each serving with a dollop of whipped cream and a fanciful chocolate shape.

Nothing's better than fresh strawberry pie, you say? How about fresh strawberry pie with a chocolate drizzle?

For a quick finish to cream puffs or eclairs, drizzle each pastry with chocolate before topping with toasted sliced almonds or pecan pieces.

Semisweet or milk chocolate (squares or bars)

EQUIPMENT:
Cutting board
Paring knife
Glass measuring cup
Small saucepan
Rubber spatula
Small resealable plastic food storage bag
Kitchen scissors
Baking sheet (for chocolate shapes)
Waxed paper (for chocolate shapes)
Small metal spatula (for chocolate shapes)

1. **For chocolate drizzles,** place chocolate on cutting board; shave it into small pieces with paring knife.

2. Place shavings in measuring cup. Fill saucepan one-quarter full (about 1 inch deep) with warm (*not hot*) water. Place measuring cup in water to melt chocolate, stirring frequently with rubber spatula until smooth. (*Be careful not to get any water into chocolate.*) Remove measuring cup from saucepan. Let chocolate cool slightly.

3. Fill plastic bag about half full with melted chocolate.

4. Seal bag securely. Cut small corner off bottom of plastic bag with scissors.

Step 1. Shaving chocolate.

Step 3. Filling bag with melted chocolate.

Step 4. Cutting small corner off bottom of bag.

Step 6. Drizzling chocolate onto dessert.

Step 9. Piping chocolate into shapes.

Step 10. Gently peeling shapes off waxed paper.

5. Position sealed end of bag in your writing hand. Position fingers near opening of bag; place other hand under bag to guide it.

6. While gently squeezing bag, guide opening just above food to drizzle chocolate, in a zigzag design, onto dessert, using an even, steady flow.

7. Stop squeezing and then lift bag at end of each design.

8. **For chocolate shapes,** prepare melted chocolate and fill plastic bag as directed in steps 1-5.

9. Invert baking sheet onto work surface; top with sheet of waxed paper. While gently squeezing bag, guide opening just above waxed paper to pipe chocolate in a steady flow, making a variety of small shapes. Stop squeezing and then lift bag at end of each shape. Create flowers, hearts, Christmas trees, lattice shapes or any lacy pattern.

10. Let stand in cool, dry place until chocolate is firm. (*Do not chill in refrigerator.*) When chocolate is firm, gently peel shapes off waxed paper using a small metal spatula. Store in cool, dry place until ready to use.

Sifted Cocoa/Sugar Designs *(Easy)*

A light dusting of powdered sugar brings out the best in spice cake, gingerbread or your favorite cheesecake.

An unfrosted nut torte just cries out for a powdered-sugar or cocoa-powder design.

Unsweetened cocoa powder or powdered sugar
Cheesecake, torte or cake

EQUIPMENT:
Kitchen scissors
Waxed paper
Doily with large pattern
Large spoon
Fine-mesh sieve
Skewers or toothpicks
Paper (for paper strips design)

1. With kitchen scissors, cut waxed paper into strips, each 2 to 3 inches wide. Tuck strips under dessert on serving plate to keep plate clean while dusting with cocoa or powdered sugar.

2. **For doily design,** place doily on top of dessert.

3. Spoon cocoa powder or powdered sugar into sieve. (Cocoa powder works well for light-colored desserts; powdered sugar is best for dark-colored desserts.)

4. Holding sieve over dessert, gently tap sieve with hand to sift cocoa powder or sugar in an even layer over entire surface.

Step 2. Placing doily on dessert.

Step 3. Spooning cocoa into sieve.

Step 4. Sifting cocoa over doily.

Step 5. Removing doily.

Step 7. Arranging paper strips on top of dessert.

5. Carefully remove waxed paper strips from around bottom edge of dessert. Remove doily from top of dessert with skewer or toothpick.

6. **For paper strips design,** omit doily. Cut clean sheets of paper into 8 to 10 strips, each strip ½ to ¾ inch wide and long enough to fit across top of surface you wish to cover.

7. Arrange paper strips in crisscross pattern on top of cake, torte or cheesecake. Continue as directed in steps 3 through 5.

Chocolate Leaves
(Intermediate)

To show off your favorite chocolate cake, place it on a pedestal cake stand. Tuck chocolate leaves around the base of the cake to create an eye-catching border.

For a dramatic cheesecake presentation, arrange three chocolate leaves in the center of your favorite cheesecake. Top the leaves with a rose of your choice—either real or one made from caramels, icing or gumdrops.

Wind up a festive meal with a light, yet elegant, dessert. Place a scoop of lemon ice or orange sherbet in a fancy dessert dish. Then add a chocolate leaf or two to each serving.

1. Place chocolate on cutting board; shave it into small pieces with paring knife.

2. Place shavings in measuring cup. Add shortening. (Use 1 teaspoon of shortening for every 2 ounces of chocolate.) Fill saucepan one-quarter full (about 1 inch deep) with warm (not hot) water.

3. Place measuring cup in water to melt chocolate, stirring frequently with rubber spatula until smooth. (Be careful not to get any water into chocolate.) Remove measuring cup from saucepan. Let chocolate cool slightly.

4. Wash leaves; dry well with paper towels. Brush melted chocolate onto underside of each leaf with paintbrush or pastry brush, coating leaf thickly and evenly. Repeat brushing with a second coating of chocolate, if desired, for a sturdier leaf.

Step 1. Shaving chocolate.

Step 3. Melting chocolate.

Step 4. Brushing backs of leaves with melted chocolate.

Semisweet chocolate (squares or bars)
Shortening
Nontoxic leaves, such as rose, lemon or camellia

EQUIPMENT:
Cutting board
Paring knife
Glass measuring cup
Small saucepan
Rubber spatula
Paper towels
Small, clean paintbrush or pastry brush
Waxed paper

5. Carefully wipe off any chocolate that may have run onto front of leaf.

6. Place leaves, chocolate side up, on waxed paper.

7. Let stand in cool, dry place until chocolate is firm. (*Do not chill in refrigerator.*)

8. When chocolate is firm, carefully peel leaves away from chocolate; chill until ready to use.

Step 5. Wiping excess chocolate off front sides of leaves.

Step 6. Placing chocolate-covered leaves on waxed paper to cool.

Step 8. Separating leaves from chocolate.

Gumdrop Bow

(Intermediate)

Festive green and red gumdrop bows add a hint of Christmas sparkle to frosted quick bread loaves. Try them on banana, date, orange or pumpkin breads.

Embellish a molded gelatin salad with a gumdrop bow in a matching or contrasting color.

Adorn the top of Boston cream pie with a pretty orange gumdrop bow.

Sugar
8 to 10 small gumdrops

EQUIPMENT:
Cutting board
Rolling pin
Paring knife

1. Sprinkle sugar on cutting board. To make a gumdrop strip, flatten eight to ten gumdrops with your thumb. Place, with ends overlapping slightly, on sugared board in two rows of four to five gumdrops each. Sprinkle gumdrops with additional sugar.

2. Roll flattened gumdrops into a 6×3-inch piece with rolling pin, turning strip over frequently to coat with sugar.

3. Trim edges of gumdrop piece with paring knife; discard edges. Cut remaining piece into ½-inch-wide strips.

4. Cut two 3-inch lengths, four 2½-inch lengths and one 1½-inch length from strips.

Step 1. Placing flattened gumdrops in overlapping rows.

Step 2. Rolling out gumdrops to completely flatten.

Step 4. Cutting strips.

5. To assemble bow, fold both 3-inch lengths in half to form two loops; place end to end to form base of bow. Press ends together to secure.

6. Fold over two of the 2½-inch lengths; place end to end on top of first loops, pressing gently to secure.

7. Wrap 1½-inch length crosswise around center of bow to conceal ends of loops. Press gently to secure.

8. Trim ends of remaining two 2½-inch lengths at an angle with knife.

9. Place these lengths under center of bow in an upside-down "V" to make ends of bow. Press gently to attach to bow.

Step 5. Placing 2 loops together to form base of bow.

Step 6. Securing top 2 loops to first layer of loops.

Step 7. Making center of bow.

Chocolate Curls
(Intermediate)

Create a halo of chocolate curls on top of your favorite frosted layer cake or cheesecake.

For an easy after-dinner treat, top cups of coffee with dollops of whipped cream and chocolate curls.

Dust chocolate curls with powdered sugar. Then use them to add a festive touch to chocolate pie or pudding.

Make brownies extra special by frosting them with vanilla buttercream frosting. Then top each brownie with a chocolate curl.

Semisweet chocolate (squares or bars)
Shortening

EQUIPMENT:
Cutting board
Paring knife
Glass measuring cup
Small saucepan
Rubber spatula
Baking pan or dish, marble slab or other heat-resistant flat surface
Metal spatula
Small metal pancake turner or cheese cutter
Small skewer or toothpick
Waxed paper

1. Place chocolate on cutting board; shave it into small pieces with paring knife.

2. Place shavings in measuring cup. Add shortening. (Use 1 teaspoon of shortening for every 2 ounces of chocolate.) Fill saucepan one-quarter full (about 1 inch deep) with warm (*not hot*) water.

3. Place measuring cup in water to melt chocolate, stirring frequently with rubber spatula until smooth. (*Be careful not to get any water into chocolate.*) Remove measuring cup from saucepan. Let chocolate cool slightly.

4. Pour melted chocolate onto back of baking pan. Quickly spread chocolate into a thin layer (about ¼ inch thick) with metal spatula.

Step 1. Shaving chocolate.

Step 3. Melting chocolate.

Step 4. Spreading melted chocolate onto back of baking pan.

5. Let chocolate stand in cool, dry place until firm. (*Do not chill in refrigerator.*) When chocolate is just firm, use small metal pancake turner, cheese cutter or paring knife to form curls. Hold pancake turner, cutter or knife at a 45° angle and scrape chocolate into a curl.

6. Using small skewer or toothpick, transfer curl to waxed paper. Store in cool, dry place until ready to use.

Step 5. Scraping chocolate into curls.

Step 6. Transferring curls.

Marzipan Cutouts/ Fruits *(Intermediate)*

For that very special occasion, create a wreath design on the top of a frosted cake or torte by arranging marzipan fruit and leaf cutouts in a ring.

Crown a strawberry, cherry or raspberry tart with a grouping of marzipan cutouts—diamonds, stars or just about any simple shape will work.

When Thanksgiving rolls around, create a delicious horn of plenty on the top of a cake by cutting the horn from rolled-out marzipan and filling the opening with marzipan fruit.

Purchased or homemade marzipan
Powdered sugar (for cutouts)

EQUIPMENT:
Small bowls
Paste or liquid food coloring
Metal teaspoons
Waxed paper (for cutouts)
Rolling pin (for cutouts)
Hors d'oeuvre or small cookie cutters (for cutouts)
Metal spatula
Hand grater (for fruits)
Paring knife or skewers (for fruits)

1. **For marzipan cutouts,** place desired amount of marzipan in a small bowl. Tint marzipan by stirring in a tiny amount of food coloring with spoon. Mix well. Add additional food coloring, a little at a time, until marzipan is desired shade.

2. Shape marzipan into a ball; flatten slightly.

3. Place marzipan between two sheets of waxed paper dusted with powdered sugar. Roll into a sheet about ⅛ inch thick with rolling pin. Discard top sheet of waxed paper.

4. Cut marzipan into desired shapes with hors d'oeuvre or cookie cutters, placing cutters as close together as possible. Carefully remove cutouts with metal spatula.

5. If desired, tint additional portions of marzipan different colors to make additional cutouts.

6. **For marzipan fruits,** divide desired amount of marzipan into small portions; place each portion in a separate bowl. Tint marzipan by stirring enough food coloring into each portion to make desired shade.

7. To make lemons, roll small pieces of yellow marzipan into ovals. Roll ovals over rough surface of grater to make markings similar to lemon peel.

Step 3. Rolling out marzipan.

Step 4. Cutting marzipan into shapes.

Step 7. Marking sides of marzipan lemons with grater.

8. Pinch both ends slightly so shapes resemble lemons.

9. To make apples or oranges, roll small pieces of red or orange marzipan into balls. Press ends to flatten slightly for top and bottom of fruit.

10. Make a dent in top and bottom of each ball with tip of paring knife or end of skewer.

11. To make leaves and stems, flatten small pieces of green marzipan to about ⅛-inch thickness with thumb. Cut out leaf shapes with knife; mark each with a leaf-vein pattern.

12. Cut out stems from remaining green marzipan. Attach a stem and leaves to top of each apple or orange, pressing gently into fruit to secure.

Step 8. Shaping ends of marzipan lemons.

Step 11. Making vein pattern in marzipan leaves.

Step 12. Attaching stems and leaves to marzipan fruit.

Gelatin / Chocolate Cutouts (Easy)

For your child's next birthday party, place a chocolate cutout alongside each serving of cake. Have the child help you by choosing the cookie or hors d'oeuvre cutter shapes he or she likes best.

Whip up treats for a Halloween party by topping frosted cupcakes with tiny orange gelatin cutouts just before serving.

Two 4-serving packages of cherry, orange or lime gelatin
1 envelope unflavored gelatin
1½ cups cranberry or apple juice
Semisweet chocolate (squares or bars, for chocolate cutouts)
Shortening (for chocolate cutouts)

EQUIPMENT:
Medium bowl
Medium saucepan
Wooden spoon
8-inch square baking pan or dish
Plastic wrap
Cutting board
Hors d'oeuvre or small cookie cutters
Small metal spatula
Baking sheet (for chocolate cutouts)
Waxed paper (for chocolate cutouts)

1. **For gelatin cutouts,** place gelatin in bowl. Pour juice into saucepan. Bring to a boil. Gradually add hot juice to gelatin, stirring with spoon until gelatin is dissolved. Cool to room temperature.

2. Line baking pan with plastic wrap, leaving enough wrap to extend over edges. Slowly pour in dissolved gelatin; chill until firm.

3. Carefully lift plastic wrap and gelatin from pan; place on cutting board.

4. Cut gelatin into desired shapes with hors d'oeuvre or cookie cutters, placing cutters as close together as possible. Carefully remove cutouts with metal spatula. Place on desired food or plate.

Step 2. Pouring gelatin into lined pan.

Step 3. Transferring gelatin to cutting board.

Step 4. Cutting out gelatin shapes.

5. **For chocolate cutouts,** omit gelatin and juice. Prepare melted chocolate as directed in Chocolate Leaves (page 66, steps 1 through 3). Let chocolate cool slightly.

6. Line baking sheet with waxed paper. Pour melted chocolate onto prepared baking sheet; quickly spread chocolate into a thin layer ($\frac{1}{8}$ to $\frac{1}{4}$ inch thick) with metal spatula.

7. Let stand in cool, dry place until chocolate is just firm. (*Do not chill in refrigerator.*) Cut chocolate into shapes with hors d'oeuvre or cookie cutters, placing cutters as close together as possible.

8. Carefully remove cutouts with metal spatula. Store in cool, dry place until ready to use.

Note: For ease in cutting chocolate cutouts, slightly warm hors d'oeuvre or cookie cutters with hands before cutting.

Step 6. Spreading chocolate in a thin layer on baking sheet.

Step 7. Cutting out chocolate shapes.

Step 8. Removing chocolate cutouts.

Feathered Sauces / Icings *(Easy)*

For truly elegant brownies or other bar cookies, frost them first with one color of frosting, then feather with a frosting of contrasting color.

Serve slices of pound cake topped with stirred custard and a feathering of strawberry or raspberry purée.

Take ice cream from simple to sophisticated. Place a scoop of your favorite ice cream on an individual serving plate. Then add a pool of chocolate sauce alongside, feathered with a drizzle of caramel or marshmallow sauce.

Desired sauce or icing
Desired sauce or icing of a contrasting color
Cake, brownies or cookies

EQUIPMENT:
Tablespoon
Dessert plates
Decorating bag or parchment cone
Decorator writing tip (No. 2, 3 or 4)
Narrow metal spatula or small knife
Kitchen scissors (optional)

1. **For feathered sauces,** spoon desired sauce onto individual dessert plates. Tilt plate to spread sauce evenly.

2. Use spoon or decorating bag fitted with writing tip to drizzle contrasting sauce* in evenly spaced parallel lines over sauce on plate (or drizzle sauce in desired design). Feather by drawing narrow metal spatula or knife through lines at regular intervals.

3. **For feathered icings,** spread desired icing over a cake or cookies of your choice using a metal spatula or knife.

4. If using a parchment cone, cut about ½ inch off bottom point of cone with scissors.

5. Position writing tip into opening in decorating bag or parchment cone. (If necessary, cut larger opening in parchment to get tip to fit.)

6. Fill bag or cone about half full with contrasting icing. Squeeze down frosting from open end of bag or cone.

7. Place open end of bag or cone in palm of your writing hand. Position fingers near opening of bag or near tip of cone. Position other hand under bag or cone to guide tip.

*Or, use melted chocolate.

Step 2. Drawing spatula through contrasting sauces to feather.

Step 3. Spreading icing on top of cake.

Step 7. Positioning filled bag in writing hand.

8. Hold bag or cone at a 45° angle just above food. While gently squeezing bag, guide tip to pipe line across top of iced cake or cookie. When you reach end of line, stop squeezing and then lift bag.

9. Repeat to pipe parallel lines.

10. Holding knife or spatula at right angle to parallel lines, draw knife through lines at regular intervals, always pulling utensil in the *same* direction.

11. Or, for a different look, *alternate* the direction in which the knife is drawn through the lines.

Step 9. Making parallel lines on top of cake.

Step 10. Feathering icing in *same* direction.

Step 11. Feathering icing in *alternating* directions.

Caramel Roses

(Intermediate)

Crown your favorite frosted layer cake with a nosegay of caramel roses.

❦

For an extra-special dessert, top petits fours with caramel roses. Serve arranged on a spectacular dessert plate.

❦

Set off a luscious caramel flan with a caramel rose.

Sugar
Purchased caramels

EQUIPMENT:
Cutting board
Teaspoon
Rolling pin
Paring knife

1. Sprinkle sugar on cutting board with spoon. Unwrap three caramels; place on sugared board. Sprinkle with additional sugar.

2. Roll each caramel into an oval (about $1/16$ inch thick) with rolling pin, turning oval over frequently to coat with sugar.

3. Cut each oval in half crosswise with paring knife.

4. To make center of rose, start at one side of a half oval and roll up to form a bud shape.

Step 2. Rolling sugared caramels into ovals.

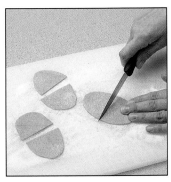

Step 3. Cutting ovals in half.

Step 4. Rolling half oval to form bud of rose.

5. To make petals, shape another half oval, straight side down, around bud.

6. Press petal to bud to secure; flare top edge slightly to resemble petal.

7. Repeat with remaining half ovals to shape additional petals, overlapping petals slightly.

8. Place rose on its side; trim off base with knife so rose will sit flat.

Step 5. Placing first petal, straight side down, around bud.

Step 6. Flaring top edge of petal.

Step 7. Forming additional petals.

Chocolate-Dipped Fruits / Nuts *(Easy)*

For the perfect ending to a rich meal, serve cups of steaming hot coffee. Garnish each saucer with a chocolate-dipped fruit or nut.

Whenever you get a yen for chocolate, make pots de crème or chocolate pudding. Then top each serving with a dollop of whipped cream and a chocolate-dipped fruit or nut.

Dress up an angel food cake by drizzling it with a chocolate glaze. Arrange chocolate-dipped fruits or nuts on top.

Semisweet or unsweetened chocolate (squares or bars)
Fresh or dried fruits
Whole or halved nuts

EQUIPMENT:
Cutting board
Paring knife
Glass measuring cup
Small saucepan
Rubber spatula
Waxed paper

1. Place chocolate on cutting board; shave it into small pieces with paring knife.

2. Place shavings in measuring cup. Fill saucepan one-quarter full (about 1 inch deep) with warm (*not hot*) water. Place measuring cup in water to melt chocolate, stirring frequently with rubber spatula until smooth. (*Be careful not to get any water into chocolate.*) Remove measuring cup from saucepan.

3. If using fresh fruit, wash and dry well. Dip fruit or nut, one at a time, into melted chocolate until chocolate coating comes about two-thirds of the way up side. Allow excess chocolate to drip off.

4. Transfer dipped fruit or nut to waxed paper. Let stand in cool, dry place until chocolate is firm. (*Do not chill in refrigerator.*)

Step 1. Shaving chocolate.

Step 3. Dipping fruit and nuts into chocolate.

Grated / Shaved Chocolate (Easy)

If you love chocolate, try this. Top squares of your favorite brownies or chocolate cake with a scoop of your favorite ice cream and a dusting of grated chocolate.

For the perfect final touch, sprinkle the top of a chocolate cream pie with shaved chocolate.

After a cold winter outing, serve up steaming mugs of hot chocolate topped with a marshmallow and a sprinkling of grated chocolate.

Semisweet or unsweetened chocolate (squares or bars)

EQUIPMENT:
Cutting board
Waxed paper (optional)
Hand grater (for grated chocolate)
Vegetable peeler (for shaved chocolate)

1. **For grated chocolate,** working over cutting board,* rub chocolate across rough surface of grater, letting pieces fall onto board.

2. If grater offers both small and large grating sections, choose section that will give the desired size pieces.

3. **For shaved chocolate,** create shavings by making short, quick strokes across chocolate with vegetable peeler.

*For easier removal of grated or shaved chocolate, cover cutting board with waxed paper before grating.

Step 1. Grating chocolate into coarse pieces.

Step 2. Grating chocolate into fine pieces.

Step 3. Shaving chocolate with vegetable peeler.

Miscellaneous Garnishes

Last, but not least, these captivating creations are fun to make and great to use as decorations. Try the egg chicken for starters!

Clockwise from top left: Butter Shapes, Tortilla Cups, Pastry Cutouts

Bacon Curls *(Easy)*

Dress up wedges of quiche with bacon curls or twists.

Use a cluster of bacon curls to decorate the top of a tossed salad or a baked casserole.

For a quick appetizer or snack, spread melba rounds or party rye bread slices with your favorite cheese spread. Top each with a bacon curl.

Bacon slices*

EQUIPMENT:
Cutting board
Paring knife
6- to 8-inch metal skewers
Broiler pan
Oven mitts
Fork
Paper towels

*Each bacon slice makes 3 curls.

1. Place bacon slices on cutting board.

2. Cut each slice crosswise into three pieces with paring knife.

3. Loosely roll up bacon pieces and thread about ½ inch apart on metal skewers.

4. Place skewers, 1½ to 2 inches apart, on unheated rack of broiler pan. Position under preheated broiler so rack is about 5 inches from heat source. Broil 4 to 6 minutes or until bacon is crisp, turning every 2 minutes.**
Cool. Carefully remove curls from skewers with fork. Drain on paper towels; cool completely.

**Skewers will be hot. Be sure to protect hands with oven mitts.

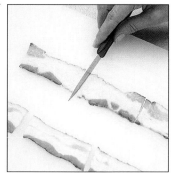

Step 2. Cutting bacon.

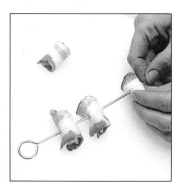

Step 3. Threading bacon onto skewers.

Step 4. Removing curls from skewers.

Tortilla Cups

(Intermediate)

Tortilla cups make great holders for guacamole, salsa or your favorite dip.

Fill tortilla cups with coleslaw or your favorite pasta salad for the perfect accent to a summer meal of grilled burgers.

For a refreshing salad, fill tortilla cups with fresh fruit pieces and drizzle with poppy seed dressing.

During the holidays, fashion small tortilla cups to hold cranberry sauce. Place filled cups around turkey on serving platter.

Cooking oil
6- or 7-inch flour tortillas

EQUIPMENT:
Large heavy saucepan
Deep-fat-frying thermometer
Oven mitts (optional)
Ladle
Long metal tongs
Paper towels

1. Pour 3 inches of cooking oil into large heavy saucepan. Attach deep-fat-frying thermometer, with bulb in oil, to side of saucepan. (Make sure bottom of thermometer does not touch bottom of pan.) Heat oil until thermometer registers 360°F.

2. Carefully place tortillas, one at a time, in hot oil. With ladle, hold tortilla down in center to form a cup. Cook tortilla until crisp and golden.

3. Empty oil from ladle; remove ladle from saucepan. Remove tortilla cup from hot oil with tongs.

4. Invert tortilla cup; drain upside down on paper towels. Repeat for desired number of tortilla cups.

Step 2. Frying tortilla.

Step 3. Removing tortilla cup from hot oil.

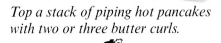

Butter Shapes *(Easy)*

Top a stack of piping hot pancakes with two or three butter curls.

At your next buffet, instead of ordinary butter pats, place molded butter or butter balls in a pretty glass bowl filled with crushed ice. Serve alongside a basket of hot muffins or biscuits.

For a hearty winter meal, top off bowls of steaming oyster stew with elegant seasoned butter rounds.

Bowl of hot water
Sticks of butter or margarine, chilled
Bowl of ice water
Chopped fresh herbs, crushed dried herbs or minced fresh garlic

EQUIPMENT:
Butter curler (for butter curls)
Butter paddles (for butter balls)
Cutting board
Paring knife
Small candy molds (for molded butter)
Metal teaspoon
Shaped butter dishes or other small dishes (for butter pots)
Small metal spatula
Fork (optional)
Small bowl
Waxed paper

1. **For butter curls,** place butter curler in hot water. Starting at far end of one butter stick, pull curler firmly across top of butter. Place finished curl in ice water. Repeat for desired amount of curls, dipping curler into hot water before starting each curl.

2. **For butter balls,** place butter paddles in ice water until cold. Place one butter stick on cutting board; cut into ½-inch pieces with paring knife.

3. Using fingers, shape butter pieces into balls. Chill until firm, if necessary.

4. Roll each ball between scored sides of paddles, moving paddles in small circles in opposite directions. Place finished butter balls in ice water.

Step 1. Pulling butter curler across stick of butter.

Step 2. Cutting butter stick into ½-inch pieces.

Step 4. Rolling balls between scored sides of paddles.

5. **For molded butter,** allow one butter stick to stand at room temperature until softened. Place candy mold in ice water until cold. Press butter firmly and evenly into mold with back of spoon; level top with knife. Chill until butter is firm.

6. Gently remove molded butter from candy mold using tip of paring knife. Place finished molded butter in ice water until ready to serve.

7. **For individual butter pots,** allow one butter stick to stand at room temperature until softened. Press butter firmly and evenly into shaped dishes with back of spoon; smooth top with metal spatula or back of teaspoon. Make decorative crisscross markings across tops with fork or paring knife, if desired.

8. **For seasoned butter,** allow one butter stick to stand at room temperature until softened. Place butter in small bowl. Add herbs or garlic; stir with spoon until well blended. (Use about 1 teaspoon fresh herbs or ¼ to ½ teaspoon dried herbs or minced garlic for each stick [½ cup] butter.) Place butter mixture on waxed paper; shape into a roll. Wrap with waxed paper; chill until firm.

9. To serve, slice butter roll into rounds with paring knife. Or, use seasoned butter roll to make butter curls or balls.

Step 6. Removing butter from molds.

Step 7. Decorating top of potted butter.

Step 8. Wrapping seasoned butter roll in waxed paper to chill.

Egg Chicken *(Easy)*

Decorate a platter of baked ham with a family of egg chickens.

❧

Make breakfast "eggstra" special for your toddlers by serving them egg chickens.

❧

Serving a chef's salad for dinner? Why not top it with an egg chicken?

Red, green or yellow bell pepper
Ripe olive slice
Hard-cooked egg, shell removed

EQUIPMENT:
Cutting board
Paring knife

1. Place bell pepper on cutting board. Cut lengthwise in half with paring knife. Remove stem, membrane and seeds; discard. Cut one 2×1½-inch rectangle from each pepper half.

2. For tail, trim both long sides of one pepper rectangle at an angle, forming a tapered rectangle. Make zigzag cuts along wide end of rectangle.

3. Cut remaining pepper rectangle in half lengthwise. For chicken's comb, cut zigzag edge along one long side of one rectangle half. If desired, trim comb to make proportional to egg.

4. Cut a small beak from remaining rectangle half; set aside.

Step 2. Cutting zigzag edge on tail.

Step 3. Trimming comb.

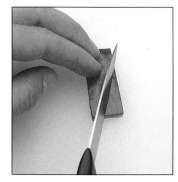

Step 4. Cutting beak.

5. For eyes, cut two tiny pieces from olive slice; set aside.

6. To assemble egg chicken, cut a long thin lengthwise slice from egg with paring knife; discard.

7. Place egg, cut side down, on cutting board. Cut a horizontal slit in wide end of egg. Insert tail, peel side up, into slit.

8. Cut a lengthwise slit in top of narrow end of egg; insert chicken's comb into slit.

9. Cut a hole in front of narrow end of egg; insert beak. Position an olive piece on either side of beak for eyes.

Step 6. Cutting slice from bottom of egg.

Step 8. Inserting comb into slit in top of egg.

Step 9. Positioning olives for eyes.

Ice Ring *(Easy)*

For an extra-special occasion, freeze edible flowers in a small ice ring and float it in a bowl of punch.

Water
Fresh edible flowers (such as dianthus, geraniums, pansies, calendulas or roses), fresh herbs or fresh fruits and nontoxic leaves (such as citrus slices, lemon leaves, halved strawberries and leaves, raspberries or nectarine slices)

EQUIPMENT:
Ring mold
Container bigger than ring mold*
Flat plate at least 1 inch larger than diameter of ring mold

*Or, use kitchen sink.

1. Add enough cold water to ring mold to just cover bottom of mold. Place mold in freezer. Freeze until surface of water is frozen. Remove from freezer.

2. Arrange half of the desired amount of flowers, herbs or fruits and leaves on ice layer in mold.

3. Carefully add enough cold water to mold to make about one-half full. Return mold to freezer. Freeze until surface of water is frozen. Remove from freezer.

4. Top with remaining flowers, herbs or fruits and leaves. Add enough cold water to fill mold to desired height. Freeze until water is completely frozen, several hours or overnight. Remove from freezer. Set mold in a bigger container. Add enough hot water to container to almost reach top of mold.

5. Let stand for a few seconds to loosen icy edges. Remove mold from container. Center plate upside down over mold. Holding mold and plate together, invert to unmold ice ring. Return to freezer until ready to use.

Step 3. Adding water to cover first layer of filled ring.

Step 5. Unmolding ice ring.

Piped Cream Cheese *(Easy)*

Squiggle cream cheese over thin slices of smoked salmon on crackers or bagel chips for the perfect accent.

Decorate whole cooked roasts by piping cream cheese in a diamond pattern over top of meat.

Pipe softened cream cheese onto your favorite gelatin salad.

Squeeze a dollop of cream cheese onto cooked steaks or hot roast beef slices.

Whipped cream cheese
Fresh dill (optional)

EQUIPMENT:
Large resealable plastic food storage bag
Large spoon
Kitchen scissors

1. Fill plastic bag about half full with cream cheese using spoon. Seal bag securely. Cut small piece off bottom corner of bag with kitchen scissors.

2. Position sealed end of bag in your writing hand. Position fingers near opening of bag; place other hand under bag.

3. **For squiggles and lines,** hold plastic bag at a 45° angle about ¼ inch from surface of food. While gently squeezing bag, guide bag to create desired design. At end of each squiggle or line, stop squeezing bag and lift away from food. Trim with fresh dill, if desired.

4. **For puffs and dollops,** hold plastic bag at a 90° angle. Position opening just above food and gently squeeze, lifting bag slightly while squeezing. When puff or dollop is desired size, stop squeezing and lift up bag. Trim with fresh dill, if desired.

Step 1. Cutting small corner off bottom of bag.

Step 3. Making squiggles.

Step 4. Making puffs.

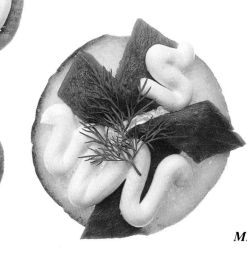

Paper Frills *(Easy)*

For a spectacular presentation, fill the center of a crown roast of pork or lamb with a mixture of colorful cooked vegetables. Trim the tip of each bone with a paper frill.

🦃

Paper frills add a touch of elegance to chicken drumsticks.

🦃

Use a large paper frill to dress up a whole bone-in ham.

White or colored paper

EQUIPMENT:
Kitchen scissors
Adhesive tape

1. For each paper frill, cut 8×4-inch rectangle from sheet of paper with scissors. Fold each rectangle in half lengthwise; fold in half lengthwise again.

2. Unfold the last fold to show crease.

3. Make cuts close together along remaining folded edge with scissors, cutting just to crease. Continue making cuts along entire length of rectangle.

Step 1. Folding paper rectangle.

Step 2. Unfolding last fold.

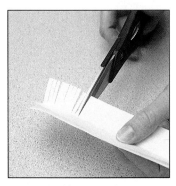

Step 3. Making cuts along folded edge just to crease.

4. Unfold paper, turn over and fold in half lengthwise.

5. Roll uncut edge of paper around index finger, allowing enough space for meat bone.

6. Secure end of paper frill with adhesive tape. Place on ends of bones just before serving.

Step 4. Refolding paper.

Step 5. Rolling uncut edge around finger.

Step 6. Taping end of frill to secure.

Pastry Cutouts (Easy)

To make a simple pie sensational, arrange a ring of star-shaped cutouts on top pie crust before baking.

For a quick alternative to a lattice-top pie, cut out several diamonds or scalloped rounds from pastry dough instead of dough strips. Arrange cutouts in a decorative pattern over pie filling before baking.

All-purpose flour
Pastry for pie crust
Milk
Sugar
Water

EQUIPMENT:
Pastry cloth
Rolling pin
Rolling pin cover (optional)
Hors d'oeuvre cutters, cookie
cutters or paring knife
Baking sheet
Metal spatula
Paring knife
Small pastry brush
Wire cooling rack
Pancake turner

1. Sprinkle pastry cloth lightly with flour. Place pastry on floured cloth; roll to about ⅛-inch thickness with rolling pin. (To minimize pastry sticking to rolling pin, use rolling pin with cloth cover.) Cut into desired shapes using hors d'oeuvre cutters, cookie cutters or paring knife.

2. **To decorate baked single-crust pie,** transfer pastry cutouts to baking sheet with metal spatula. Use tip of paring knife to decorate cutouts with design, if desired. Brush cutouts with milk using pastry brush; sprinkle with sugar.

3. Bake cutouts at 425°F (or at temperature given in pastry recipe) until golden brown. Transfer to wire rack with pancake turner; cool. Arrange baked cutouts on top of pie filling.

4. **To decorate unbaked double-crust pie,** remove cutouts from pastry cloth with metal spatula. Use pastry brush to brush back side of cutouts with water. Arrange cutouts, moistened side down, on top crust of pie.

5. Cut slits in top crust with paring knife as part of design. Or, cut slits along edge of cutouts. Brush crust and cutouts with milk; sprinkle with sugar. Bake as directed in pie recipe.

Step 2. Decorating cutouts with desired pattern.

Step 3. Placing cutouts on pie.

Step 5. Cutting slits in crust.